A Journey In
Massage

A Journey In
Massage

What You Should Know Before You Book
Your Next Massage Appointment

IRMA ROMANO

Photos by Florent and Maxime Courty

Poems by Juno Cristi

BALBOA.
PRESS

A DIVISION OF HAY HOUSE

Balboa Press books may be ordered through booksellers or by contacting:

Balboa Press
A Division of Hay House
1663 Liberty Drive
Bloomington, IN 47403
www.balboapress.com
1-(877) 407-4847

Because of the dynamic nature of the Internet, any web addresses or links contained in this book may have changed since publication and may no longer be valid. The views expressed in this work are solely those of the author and do not necessarily reflect the views of the publisher, and the publisher hereby disclaims any responsibility for them.

The author of this book does not dispense medical advice or prescribe the use of any technique as a form of treatment for physical, emotional, or medical problems without the advice of a physician, either directly or indirectly. The intent of the author is only to offer information of a general nature to help you in your quest for emotional and spiritual well-being. In the event you use any of the information in this book for yourself, which is your constitutional right, the author and the publisher assume no responsibility for your actions.

Certain stock imagery © Thinkstock.
Any people depicted in stock imagery provided by Thinkstock are models, and such images are being used for illustrative purposes only.

ISBN: 978-1-4525-6153-0 (e)
ISBN: 978-1-4525-6152-3 (sc)

Printed in the United States of America

Balboa Press rev. date: 11/7/2012

CONTENTS

Light of Seasons

I stand alone in time and space
With no land, no color, no race
The rock that you have stumbled on
The shell that whispers wind and song
I watch the eagle as it flies
And gaze upon eternal skies
I am the bridge that you have crossed on
Or a wave that meets the ocean
My mind has leaped to higher places
Stopping every fear it faces
I witnessed every raging storm
Taking heavy shape and form
I walked the road where no one goes
And found the spring where bounty flows
I chose the path away from reason
And let my light guide through all seasons
I came to rest one autumn's dawn
And found you dancing by the lawn
And little did I know in time
The light I saw was yours not mine

DEDICATION

This book is dedicated to all the healers and body workers on the planet that have touched the hearts and souls of so many with their hands and spirit. Unlike any other profession massage therapists have the ability to touch a person on many levels not just their bodies. The one that are in touch with their inner beings and can see the bigger picture have a profound effect on the person they are treating and the Universe as a whole. We never seem to stop learning this mystical planet and the human species as quantum physics helps us also understand more and more each day the manifested and the manifested the miracle of life that we all are. My search for answers to being whole and not perfect but able to have the power to heal ourselves through massage and holistic living is an ongoing process, one that takes me around the world exploring and storytelling in hopes to inspire others to ask the same questions for themselves.

I dedicate this book to all the people who have paste away from cancer in the last few years, friends, teachers, family members. This book is for you and for Wellness. Special thanks to Juno Cristi for her poems and her powerful presence with words and to Florent Courty for allowing the Source to work so magically through is photography.

Namaste.

INTRODUCTION

"All change is not growth, as all
movement is not forward."
~Ellen Glasgow

Over the last twenty years, massage therapy has been increasingly in demand and rising in popularity amongst people from all walks of life here in Canada and internationally. The word "Spa" and "Massage" is seen everywhere from magazines, books, the internet, television, and in the media across the world. Never before have we seen so many spas, resorts, wellness centers, and clinics being established offering massage therapy to the masses as well as different kinds of body treatments such as "Chocolate Wraps, "Wine Therapy," "Mud Treatments" just to name a few. In Israel, one can get a Snake Massage by having snakes crawl on your back. In New York, people are lining up for pigeon poop facials and in Austria you can order a leech treatment as well. These are bizarre spa treatments from around the world and even the airports and malls as well as convention centers are taking part in this new trend which has only been rising in popularity year after year. The question is, "What does it all mean?" How do we decipher amongst the "Massage Lingo" and know what exactly what works and what doesn't? What would you sign up for?

We are now offering massage therapy in destination spas, resorts, wellness retreats. Everyone can take part in the experience from teenagers, children, men and women of all ages. This new trend of enjoying a vacation and relaxing at the same time by booking a spa appointment is on the rise and is now mainstream. If you are looking for a retreat getaway you can Google the word "retreat" and a long list of treatments will come up.

You can get away and have anything from your numerology read, sip green drinks all weekend and visit a Shaman or hike in the woods, to going for yoga and a massage weekend in search for your inner child or practice a "Vision Quest". There are literally thousands of different packages being offered here in our own backyard. Aside from these packages that one can choose from and use to rejuvenate and feel like they are more connected with themselves, I would like to focus on how massage therapy is used for leisure as well as medical purposes, making it a profession of choice amongst a wide range of people in our society.

With the increase of offices, jobs and computer work, so has the demand for massage therapy. Contrary to popular belief, the increase of technology has not made the work hours decrease or easier for most families. In fact it has made the work hours longer. Many companies have increased the work load for a single worker cutting back on staff and increasing the stress factor for many individuals. We live in a world where technology is taking over how we do business and communicate with each other and we are now seeing the effects it has on our bodies and health.

Massage Therapy is being covered by insurance companies in Canada for workers that are in need of stress reduction, and focused clinical attention due to related work environment.

Many couples are also finding themselves juggling work, raising kids, keeping the house in order and finding that there are not enough hours in the day to do everything on the agenda. The average Canadian woman with children is facing long hours in the office and additional work when she goes home which entails child rearing and house work. Luckily, as

Canadians, many of us are insured through work coverage for massage therapy through our work yet many of you do not know that you are actually covered or do not use your coverage.

This shows that many corporations do recognize that stress in the workforce and its effects on productivity amongst workers. Part of the benefits offered to these employees is massage therapy. Some of the professions that have massage therapy coverage are teachers, police officers, firemen, and bankers justto name a few. Everyone can benefit from massage therapy to correct posture, eliminate stress, increase circulation, using it as part of a wellness program like yoga classes to and improving their quality of life.

As a Registered Massage Therapist I have gathered questions from working with clients over the years and decided that we needed to better understand the world of Massage, Spas, and Retreats. From observing and having worked in different venues I wanted to help the Canadian public to clear some basic information and most asked questions. This guide was developed as a result to answer your most frequently asked questions and to also give you the tools and information you need to make massage therapy a conscious choice for wellness and to avoid some pitfalls that are too common when booking a spa appointment. This book will help you make informed decisions and take the myths you might have heard surrounding the profession of massage therapy.

The one question I have been asked over the years repeatedly is, "Why did you decide to become a massage therapist?" and "Do you enjoy being a massage therapist?" Now these questions are asked while my clients are in my treatment room face down on their stomach and for some reason it always catches me by surprise when I hear the question being asked. The truth is I rarely sit down and ponder about this choice. But it is a valid question. One that deserves an honest answer, and yet the answer is not simple and it also takes me back in time.

I graduated from Massage Therapy School in Toronto back in 2004 at Kikkawa College, a private massage school that offered a two year massage program. After reviewing my choices of schools in Toronto and touring different locations at some of the top massage schools in the city, I decided that Kikkawa was well suited for me based on the welcoming atmosphere from very first day I went into the registration office. All my life decisions and my life events up until that point had led me into the massage world for various reasons.

As a young girl my dream had always been to be in show business and perform on stage. After years of studying acting, dance, and singing I often found work as a bartender or waitress while I went out to do auditions. I have to admit that waiting on tables and bartending was never my forte and I needed to have something I was passionate about to fall back on. I was a person who enjoyed working with my hands versus sitting at a desk for long hours. I had worked in banks, in offices and as a flight attendant but my personality really lent itself to variety and physicality with a combination of creativity. For some reason, I was the type of person who needed to be active in her work environment. I also considered becoming a chef several times due to my passion for cooking and food. But upon deep reflection and consideration, massage therapy seemed like the best choice for me. I was looking for an unconventional way to make a living and I also believed that success went hand in hand with passion. Money was never a driving force or a priority when it came to making a career decision which was why I had chosen theater and not law school. I knew that in order to survive spiritually I had to have passion and a sense of accomplishment when waking up in the morning which also meant feeling excited about the day that was ahead of me. Life was too short to waste by doing a job I did not enjoy just for the sake of the mighty dollar. I had a creative mind and in order to go on auditions I needed to have a flexible schedule but the real reason for my journey into massage school really began as far back as 1994.

During that year I was studying acting in the United States and one afternoon while I was driving down a country road on my way to a friend's house, I was hit by a car and I crashed my vehicle on the side of the road but was able to walk away in one piece. That accident led me into a year of rehabilitation and constant medical care. I was unable to finish my courses at the local University and decided to focus instead in recovery. I had multiple health care professionals looking after me that year. During my recovery process from a moderate whiplash injury I was seeing physiotherapists, chiropractors, doctors, and a number of specialists, you name it. I was at the clinic twice a week for what seemed a never ending process to recovery or insanity.

After the first three months of rehabilitation I became depressed and my medication was making me feel worse not better. It was during my visits to the doctor that I was introduced to a very talented registered massage therapist who brought me back to health in a way that no other occupational therapist did. It was also my first time getting a massage and I was nervous not knowing what to expect. She explained to me how to get on the massage table and what she would be treating during the hour. Her massage table was very comfortable and I was covered in sheets and a warm blanket the entire time. It was the only therapy that I looked forward to and refused to miss. I saw her once a week for three months and slowly was able to stop taking my medication and get back into the workforce enjoying my life once again. I really owe my massage profession to the accident and to one talented massage therapist.

Not long after, I decided to move from the Niagara region to Toronto and regained my ability to function by joining a gym, working full time, getting an agent for my acting career and being part of life once again. It was a new beginning in a new city and I enjoyed every moment of my new life.

Having been injured in a car accident and experiencing massage therapy had left an impression on me so much so that the desire to become one myself and to help others get back on their feet was a serious consideration. I know first hand how it feels to be in a position of chronic pain and not seeing the light at the end of the tunnel. Your mind can play tricks on you and make you believe you are a victim. Depression sets in, creating a downward spiral that can cripple you if you allow it.

The road to recovery for me meant getting off this merry go round by waving good bye to the pain killers I was on, and getting regular massages, with the combination of a workout program I had designed for myself at the gym. It was my car accident that gave me a new lease on life and made me appreciate the power of touch. It also taught me the power to heal was always within me. Once I released the labels from the medical profession like "Fibromyalgia," and being fed pills that were making me emotionally sick, I was on the road to recovery and that was a very powerful experience.

So to answer the question, "Why did you become a massage therapist?", for me it was a desire to help others, knowing I enjoyed working with my hands, and having a flexible schedule that would enable me to peruse a creative life on the side. Yet it wasn't until the year of 2004 that I decided to give massage therapy school a try. Between 1994 and 2004 I had a series of life experiences that entailed a marriage that lasted two years, followed by a divorce. Once I put my failing marriage behind me, I was ready for a new beginning and being single again was a great opportunity to dedicate myself to a new career. I had a number of unsatisfying jobs over the years. Nothing made me feel alive and happy anymore. That is when I decided that massage therapy was going to be my profession. Sometimes you have plans for yourself but the universe has another path for you instead and so you have to have an open mind and heart and go with the flow.

In the fall of 2004, I was in massage school full time. It was an exciting process but also a difficult one financially as well as academically. I had not been a student since graduating from high school and college in the early nineties. This was also a science based course and anatomy was a foreign language to me.

Nothing could have prepared me for what was ahead in terms of learning, and the hours I had to put into my studies. It was the hardest two years of my life. On average I studied four hours every night, seven days a week. Sometimes, more hours depending on what type of exam I was preparing for. The practical exams where always harder and took longer hours to study and rehearse. I had a great support system with a group of students. I would not have been able to get through some of the toughest times in those two years without my study group. I was also blessed with outstanding teachers and school personnel that offered constant support and encouragement. My two years of schooling taught me that I had what it took to learn and get through some of the toughest exams in a health care program. The second year of school was the toughest leaving me with three bouts of shingles in one month. I found out what the word stress meant the summer of 2006.

Yet, it was what I experienced after I graduated from massage school that left me unsatisfied and wondering if I had made the right choice. As a registered massage therapist, I have had the pleasure of treating clients for the last five years and using all of my skills and knowledge in a way that was satisfying and very rewarding depending on where I was working at the time. The workforce had many obstacles I was not aware of before entering massage school and felt that two worlds were colliding. This book was created as a result of wanting to share this experience with all of you.

Behind the scenes, most of you will never really get to see or even be aware of what can happen in a spa or other venue unless you read about it in a guide like this one. I have put together my five years of work experience to share with all of you in hopes you can all get a general idea of what massage therapy entails. This is a guide that will open your eyes to the real world of massage therapy in Canada.

I have answered some of the most frequently asked questions that have been brought up during my treatments with my clients. I want to prepare you and give you the tools you need to make your next massage appointment a great experience. Maybe you have health benefits and have never used them before because of the fear of the unknown and mystery that surrounds massage therapy. Maybe you are an avid massage goer but are not aware of the entire picture when it relates to massage and choosing a massage therapist. Either way, this information was gathered to help you decide if massage therapy is the right choice for you or your family and how to avoid the pitfalls that so many make when booking a massage appointment.

Many of you out there will make an appointment to get a massage based on flyers you have seen somewhere. The ones that show a picture of a woman on her stomach with stones placed on her back. They conjure images of peace, tranquility, and pampering. You might have seen this online or at a local spa or resort or found them in your mailbox or the cover of a spa magazine. But how many of you know what a registered massage therapist really is? I have been asked many times by clients. "So how many years does it take to become a massage therapist?" Most of you do not know what the Canadian standards for massage therapy are, and why you should unless you are heading out to massage school yourself and have a career in the profession.

In this Canadian massage guide, I will break it all down in the chapters ahead for you so that you have a basic understanding of the process and schooling in the profession which also varies from province to province. This is important and relevant information to know and you should also be made aware that not all countries have the same standards when it comes to massage therapy, in fact not all of the Canadian provinces follow the same rules either.

The massage therapy program is very different from country to country, and from province to province. In the United States for example a massage course can be five hundred hours or more depending on what state the student is in. In Canada, becoming a massage therapist varies depending on what province the student is attending. The following provinces require the massage student to take a board exam after graduation and are regulated by the province as a way to protect the public from negligence and to make sure the massage therapist keeps their skill level up to date.

British Columbia has a requirement of 3,000 hours of studies which makes the course a three to four year program. This is one of the highest standards for massage schooling in Canada. Next we have Ontario, Newfoundland, and Labrador who require the student to be registered with 2,200 hours of studies. The other provinces also require 2,200 hours but are not registered and regulated while Quebec standards are at 400 hours of schooling which ranks that province with the lowest standards. As you can see going from one province to another can get quite complicated for a massage therapist if they want to move to another province and continue to work as a massage therapist.

If you are overseas in a different country the standards will be different depending on where you are traveling. Canada along with France and Germany has one of the highest educational standards at the moment for massage therapy education and the students in these counties are in demand internationally. Upon graduation the ability to get a job in the United States or Europe are very high for Canadian massage therapists that have studied in Ontario and British Columbia or any province that is regulated. Many resorts from the United States come to Canada to recruit and hire Canadian massage therapists upon graduation. Canadian massage therapists are recruited by cruise ships and ski resorts from the United States right after being registered. For many younger massage therapists this is a great opportunity to travel and make money at the same time.

The massage therapy program that I studied under in Ontario covered a two year course load that included anatomy, pathology, kinesiology, manual skills, massage techniques, clinical sciences, orthopedics, remedial exercise, hydrotherapy, and the treatment of chronic diseases, injuries, with the choice of two electives. My two years in massage school included Thai Massage, Sports Massage, and two years of clinic, marathons, volunteer work at a physiotherapy clinic, and a placement in a HIV clinic downtown Toronto as well as an exposure to treating clients with MS and Parkinson. Needless to say, I went home late and woke up early seven days a week for two years. My social life was non-existent and the only focus in my life for those two years was studying massage therapy. For me it also meant giving up working as I found that school was too hard for me to continue working even part-time.

All of the massage schools are based on Swedish massage. Many of you out there get confused about what type of massage you will be receiving and part of this confusion comes from the spa menu that you come across but I will get to that later in other chapters. Once a student has graduated and passed the board exams here in Ontario for example they can add more classes, techniques, and are required to do so as part of the continuing education requirements. While massage school gives you a great foundation on treating conditions and knowing pathologies it does not make you an expert in different types of massages. We spend a week learning certain types of techniques such as TMJ or Pregnancy massage yet nothing in detail to make us experts in all areas. It would take a few more years of schooling to cover all the bases when it comes to different types of massages. More courses are needed to really fully understand on a deeper level any other modality and each therapist has a passion for something different. For example I have no desire of furthering my knowledge on TMJ massage which entails sticking your fingers in someone's mouth. It is effective but someone else might find it very interesting. Some will gravitate towards treating athletes, others will focus on working in a spa only while other therapist only enjoys the clinical setting and helping accident victims or injured clients recover faster. In general, the therapist's hobbies and personality lends itself to gravitating towards what they find appealing and interesting with the physical capacity of doing the work.

In Ontario the CMTO sends the registered massage therapist a list that they must fill out showing courses taken every three years. In British Columbia that requirement is every two years. For example one can add cranial sacral, sports massage, pregnancy massage, and many other skills along the way. You must also show that you are keeping up with your anatomy and pathology knowledge and also taking other classes and workshop that relate to health and massage therapy. Failure to show the CMTO your continuing education will result in the licensing of the therapist being revoked.

Massage therapists will pay an average of seven hundred dollars a year in Ontario to be able to keep their license to practice and liability insurance that covers them for three million dollars in case of a law suit or injury to the client. The renewal is done every year at the same time for every registered massage therapist in the month of November.

The CMTO is the college of massage therapy of Ontario and governs the standards and quality assurance for the province. The cost of massage school and being in practice is extremely high. On average massage school is twelve thousand dollars a semester not including wage loss for the two years, and equipment, board exams, and continuing education. The CMTO protects the public against negligent massage therapist and has a very high standard for health and safety. This will be covered in depth in other chapters.

I know that for any of us who set out to take on any program, career, or course the reality of the work that it entails will clash with the dream that one has in their mind. Nothing could have prepared me for what was ahead in the real world compared to the information that was given to me in massage school. Although I enjoyed knowledgeable teachers and had a great support system in school, looking back now I am not always certain I would do the program again knowing what it takes to keep my license updated and how hard the road to success can be. In the end all my sacrifices and hard work had paid off but the world of massage therapy was not the one I had envisioned while in I was a student. What I saw and experiences during the last five years working in my profession is what I want to share with all of you.

Sojourn

I want to travel to a place
I have never been
To a land no one has ever seen
Beyond the fog
and the dark clouds
Or go past the mangroves
and the distant lakes
So I can turn shadows
into stardust

CHAPTER ONE

The Journey Into The Massage World

"Seeing ahead is fun. But pushing
forward is very hard work."

Bonnie Purdden

In the fall of 2006, I received my license as a registered massage therapist
and landed my first job in the west end of the city of Toronto. I worked
with two former Kikkawa students that had been in the business
and working for themselves for ten years. They had a great operation
and serviced the people of the community and were well respected.
I was working on commission which is what many clinics in the city
offered most massage therapists. At the time, the pay rate in Canada
for registered massage therapists was on a decline while the price for an
hour massage increased steadily. I was on a 60/40 split which seemed
like a decent wage at the time until you find yourself onsite for eight
hours with only one to two treatments coming your way. One thing
massage school does not really prepare you for is how to negotiate a
work contract and what you should be asking for in terms of wages.
The massage therapy profession is still ill-defined and without any
union or base salary rate unlike nurses or other health care professions
in the country. The RHPA regulates all licensed health care providers

in Ontario which includes Doctors, Nurses, Physiotherapist, Massage Therapists and many others while the CMTO protects the public against the negligence of massage therapists and does not promote the profession.

Many students believe they will be swimming in money and abundance after they graduate, believing that the pay rate will be over and above what they could ever earn in another profession. This can be a reality only if they open up their own practice and are great business people. Not everyone wants the responsibility of marketing or building a business right after they graduate or ever down the road for that matter. The road to success is long and requires a set of skills that you need to acquire with time and effort.

Male therapists have a harder time getting booked due to gender preferences by clients. They also will experience a harder path to creating success for themselves finding out that many employers will pass them by due to gender. The men I have seen succeed in massage therapy run their own business and hire massage therapist to work for them. One male therapist from my school was retired in his twenties and sold his spa in the city of Toronto. He literally retired at an early age due to his drive and ambition.

Men do not like massages from males and females feel uncomfortable as well. In the massage world one needs to wear a business hat and really negotiate before settling in a work place. Without a business mind massage therapy becomes frustrating and not a very lucrative way to make a living. In general massage therapist are forced to have several part-time jobs to make ends meet.

In my first year of being out in the work force in my field I had worked in six different locations. I struggled with paying bills, rent, food, transportation and this went on for years. I sat in clinics, spas, wellness centers on a commission base folding towels for free, doing chair massage for free, and getting nowhere fast. If I was on salary I was making anywhere from ten dollars an hour to twenty-three dollars an hour never having any health benefits, or labor law protection if I was dismissed or needed unemployment insurance. Like most of my colleagues I was working at three different locations struggling to make a decent wage and not being able to cover my living expenses. This was a far cry from my vision as a student in massage school.

The worst paying jobs in the city were in the very posh neighborhoods in spas that charged the clients top dollar and had an endless list of VIP's and Celebrity clientele. These spas paid the therapist anywhere from minimum wage to twenty-three dollars an hour. All of a sudden my bartending years seemed extremely appealing to me. There was no other profession out there that could actually make you work for free for hours while you waited for a client to walk in. The spa industry was one of the greediest of all establishments and one of the worst work environments for the massage therapist for various reasons. Not only did my clinical skills not get utilized but in five years of working as a registered massage therapist I had worked in twenty-two different locations ranging from spas, resorts, clinics, and wellness centers. In some places I lasted two days in others I was there for less than a year. I was fired twice and quit the other twenty times.

Here are some of the reasons for my terminations and leaving these different places.

1. I refused to double up on the sheets on the massage bed preferring to wipe down the massage tables instead.
2. I was verbally abused by a twenty-one year old a aesthetician who was a manager because she was drinking all day.
3. I was terminated after a year of service in High Park because my shoes were the wrong color.
4. On Avenue Road in a posh spa, I complained that the bulk of the massages where being given to the a aesthetician and I did not like sitting in the staff room folding towels on a commission based salary.
5. I complained to the owner of a high end spa in Yorkville that the health history forms were non-existent and needed to be organized.

6. I was verbally abused in the same spa by the manager because I had nine treatments back to back with a five minute break in between clients with no lunch break and apparently I was not doing enough to clean up the waiting area. I was also supposed to pick up dirty glasses and dishes that were left behind clients. The exact words from the manager were. "You don't do much to help out around here!" That was my last day at work in that spa.

7. On Yonge and Bloor I worked in a high end spa for ten dollars an hour and made two hundred and fifty dollars a week doing fifteen massages a week.

8. I overheard the owner of a spa tell the receptionist to not give me a hot stone massage treatment when it could be given to an a aesthetician instead for less pay. Yet I had already been asked to show up at eight am that morning to perform the treatment.

9. The chiropractor that hired me in their clinic was taking my referred clients telling them they did not need a massage but they should do ART instead. I waited all day for a walk-in client making no hourly wage.

10. I had to chase owners of spas and clinics to get paid sometimes taking me as long as four weeks sometimes my checks bouncing several times.

11. Favoritism and co-workers taking my massages by going to the computer at the front desk and moving treatment for themselves or talking my request.

There are other reasons why I left these working conditions behind. Other times I was promised that the spa or clinic was busy and that I would do well but the reality was I often ended up unable to cover my rent and expenses? When my taxes where due at the end of the year and I had to cover the expenses of doing business and a school debt that was still lingering, massage therapy under those conditions was not worth my time and effort. I was underpaid and burnt out, sometimes suffering physical pain in my neck, wrists, hands, and low back.

But the biggest scars was being underappreciated, sometimes humiliated, and viewed as a commodity by some of these spa owners and managers. The lack of respect that was thrown in my direction was at times too much to handle and after five years of being a massage therapist I had gained forty extra pounds as a result of my unhappiness. I often wanted to quit my profession and perhaps go back to school and become a chef or start my own business in another profession.

Remember as a client you will pay anywhere from eighty-five dollars for an hour massage at the spa to one hundred and fifty if not more. Your massage therapist will not see half of that money at the end of the day. It will remain in the pocket of the spa with the pretense that the overhead and the cost of doing business justifies paying the therapist minimally.

The spa industry takes advantage of younger massage therapist that is fresh out of school.Many of these kids are still living at home and believe that making twenty dollars an hour is reasonable as it is their first job. But when you have to live in a city like Toronto and make ends meet spending forty thousand dollars on a career and not making at least fifty dollars an hour for the skill and physical labor that comes with massage therapy it is an injustice. For that reason, many massage therapists leave the profession after two years of being in practice and move on to greener pastures, seeking job security which is hard to find in the massage industry.

Many massage therapists are forced to take on a second career to secure stability and income. Contrary to popular belief by the public, most spas are not a tranquil oasis to work in for the most part. It is a toxic, negative vortex that takes advantage of therapists, and the clients that attend. Many of the massage therapist and aesthetician that work in these places are extremely unhappy and are being burnt out physically working minimum wage without job security.

It is impossible to plan a future when you have no idea where your next pay check is coming from and how much it will be. Some weeks are good and other weeks you haven't made enough to cover your expenses.

Starting a business is risky but when you are working for others and you are not living well then taking the risk and starting a business makes more sense. If you get a treatment by someone who is not happy with their work environment and they are burnt out and you happen to be client number nine, do you think they really care if you are safe, that the room is sanitized, and that you will get one hundred percent of their attention?

In 2009 I made the conscious decision to leave the city of Toronto and move to Niagara-on-the-Lake. That same year I worked in my neighborhood of Toronto in a spa that had just been opened for not even two weeks. It was called Jung Spa and was located in Riverdale in the east end of the city.I never saw my first paycheck from the establishment. The RCMP was confiscating laptops, and shutting down the operation the week I was due for my pay. Jung Spa was opened by a Korean woman in her early twenties and her fiancé who was in his mid-forties from East Europe the spa owners were being arrested for stealing over half a million dollars from a spa downtown Toronto. They had stolen credit card number and debit card information from rich clients and waited six months to spend the money which funded Jung Spa, a condo in Yorkville, and a very rich lifestyle. It was not long before the story was plastered all over the news, papers, and online. I had worked at the spa for three weeks and never saw a penny for my hard work which really forced me to leave the city in search for peace and stability.

In the small town of Niagara-on-the-Lake the same work ethics that was seen too many times in spasacross the city was being repeated. My life and what seemed like paradise in a small quite town surrounded by vineyards and flowers quickly became hell and in less than a year I was off looking for a better place to practice massage therapy once again.

In the five years of practicing massage I had wanted to quit the profession several times due to lack of finances, and abusive work environment that I so often found myself in. I was not alone in my frustrations in the work force many of my colleagues went through the same frustrations as I did, others settled for a low wage not really looking at what they were worth. Others worked for themselves and found great satisfaction as a massage therapist never setting foot in a spa. With massage therapy there was so many paths and decisions to make along the way. Not all registered massage therapists will have this kind of experience but in general many do. It is one of those careers that can be rewarding when the therapists takes control of the work environment and diversifies and has strong boundaries and self-esteem.

Looking back I realize that my boundaries were weak for the most part. It wasn't until later that I reached out and received the knowledge and help I needed from other well established massage therapists and I was I able to break free of a dead end cycle. I was aware that I was creating this life and the unnecessary struggle so I took couching sessions from a successful massage therapists and that is when things turned around for me. It was up to me to make the life I wanted happen. I was good at my work and enjoyed touching the lives of so many people. The look on my client's faces at the end of a session is what kept me going along the way.

Without the business mind I would not be able to break free of these corporate sweat shops that called themselves spas. I needed to have control of hygiene, music, my clients comfort, I needed to listen to their problems and help them achieve wellness. I wanted to be able to give remedial exercises after a massage and serve my clients a tea or a glass of water without rushing them out the door denying them a shower afterwards and saying a sentence over and over again like a broken record which so many other massage therapists did. I was not a robot and neither where my clients I needed to bond with them and have a professional relationship with them. I wanted to stop giving a cookie cutter massage and start thinking outside the box.

A Reverie

So here we are in cosmic dance
A taste of Spring, A new romance
While secret gardens come to life
A reverie awaits in mine
We walk in paths all paved with leaves
We dance with spirits in this eve
The hour bequeaths a time to rest
And we lay down our sacred nest
What sleeps beneath this peaceful Earth
A golden light, a soul rebirth
So here we are in cosmic dance
A taste of Spring, a new romance
While secret gardens come to life
A reverie awaits in mine

CHAPTER TWO

Behind the Soft Music and Waterfalls

"Pain is inevitable.
Suffering is optional."

M.Katheleen Casey.

Behind the water falls and soft music is a world of drama that the public rarely gets to see. After working in the spa industry as a massage therapist in Ontario mostly Toronto, Niagara region and the Muskoka districts I decided to share with the public myobstacles whichI faced on a regular basis. The decision to make you aware of what actually goes on behind closed doors was to help move the professionforward and help raise the standards in spas and centers that offer massage across the country.

Most spas and other establishments do not follow health regulations putting the public at risk of catching infectious diseases. The spa environment can become one of the most dangerousplaces if not sanitized properly. In a pedicure and manicure area there are over three hundred different kinds of bacteria and viruses. Do not be fooled by the websites with the beautiful pictures of a woman lying on her stomach with three big stones on her back and a flower on her head enjoying the touch of a massage therapist by a water fall or the "Best Spa" list off Google engine. I have seen firsthand and have worked in these places that were nominated

"Top Spa" the devastating effects of what can happen when staff and management do not care for your safety or the spread disease such as hepatitis or a skin infection on your face or fungus on your toe nail.

The spa industry makes big money by squeezing in nine to eight treatments with five minutes breaks in between clients with seven or more massage therapists working hour on the hour. At a price tag of one hundred and twenty dollars an hour that makes them anywhere from five to eight thousand dollars a day not including other treatments and aesthetics. Their bottom line is making money without any regard for you or their staff. This is what I have witnessed for myself in the last five years but not all places are created equal.

Most massage places I have worked in break health and safety regulations on a regular basis. Out of the twenty-two spas and clinics I have worked in maybe two had massage table spray bottles in all the rooms most managers did not order table spray and did not have it available. I often brought in my own disinfectant spray and oils but was mostly reprehended for it and told not to bother bringing in my own equipment into work.

In Niagara-on-the-lake with the approval of the manager, staff would layer sheets on top of each other to and make clients lay on top of dirty perspired sheets from previous clients. This was justified by the fact that there were eight to nine treatments a day booked with only a five minute break between bookings. Time was money and there was no time to waste. Hot stones were wiped down with Lysol wipes and not soaked in water after a treatment. This is typical in most spas because there is no down time for proper equipment cleaning in most places. Plastic glasses are hand washed by staff in a sink where sandals are also being washed. Most of the time the manager knew a health inspector was on their way and lied through the inspections. They never see the layered sheets, tables not being wiped down, the over booking, aesthetician leaving their tools half covered in disinfectant liquid making spreading disease a high risk factor. Massage therapists work even if they have a cold and are contagious some have been fired for not wanting to come in to work when they were seriously contagious. The list of infractions is long and unfortunately the health inspections are lacking in the spa industry.

I have seen the devastating consequences of low hygienic standards in the workplace. From staff suffering bacterial infection on their faces from a facial treatment leaving them disfigured and on heavy medication that took over a year to cure a skin condition that left them with an immune deficiency problem in the long run. I have also witnessed nail fungus that are permanent and cannot be treated due to the lack of proper equipment disinfecting procedures. With a pill costing the client five hundred dollars with no guarantee of killing toe fungus the fifty dollar pedicure becomes very expensive.

In the city of Toronto many nail places had to be shut down due to the spread of diseases and we are now starting to see these nail salons using disposable tools.This is also true of a Tattoo parlor that was shut down for using used needles and spreading hepatitis virus in the city of Toronto. The truth of the matter is in a public place like a spa with hot tubes which are often not wiped down properly either exposes you to a variety of bacteria and illness. It is a public place and hundreds of clients are walking in and everyday seven days a week. It is only now that we see Health Canada getting more strict and passing laws that will keep the public safe from unscrupulous practices from greedy owners who have no regard for your safety. But for some people these laws come a little too late. Here is an article that was published in June 29th of 2011.

Nail salons under the microscope
MARIANA IONOVA
METRO TORONTO
Published: *June 29, 2011 10:31 p.m.*
Last modified: *June 29, 2011 10:37 p.m.*

A manicurist meticulously removes the cuticles from your fingernails, while her colleague applies glistening polish on your flawless, sandal-ready toes. The thought that the footbath might not have been disinfected doesn't even cross your mind.

But less-than-perfect sanitary conditions in some nail salons could result in growth of dangerous bacteria and transmission of viruses, according to Dr. Allison McGeer, infectious disease consultant at Mount Sinai Hospital.

The city currently has no official licensing and regulation procedures for nail salons. Earlier this month, Toronto Health put forth recommendations for a bylaw requiring all tattoo parlours, piercing salons and beauty spas to apply for a licence, undergo initial inspection and display their inspection results in their front entrance. If approved, it will be implemented next year.

"(Infections) are usually not life-threatening but they can be very persistent and quite annoying" said McGeer, adding that these can range from mild skin irritations to Hepatitis C.

Toronto Public Health inspects nail salons once a year but, because there is no registration system, officials have no way of knowing when a new business starts up.

"Part of the issue is that we need to find places early on in their operation so that we can educate operators when they start out instead of finding them haphazardly through the inspection program," said Dr. HerveenSachdeva, of Toronto Public Health.

The public does not see what goes on behind closed doors and if they did they would think twice about spending hundreds of dollars on treatments at the spa with the notion they are being looked after. In 1994 fifty people contracted legionnaire's disease a sometime fatal form of pneumonia due to a whirlpool spa bath on a cruise ship. The media often times hides these stories so that people continue to feel like public hot tubes and spas are safe. Nothing kills a business like bad publicity. I no longer get pedicures unless my own equipment is being used and it is only because I have worked in close proximity to aesthetician where I observed tools not being soaked properly, or equipment and creams for facials left on the floor where everyone is walking with their outdoor shoes. I do not risk the chances of getting a toe fungus or virus or skin diseases on my face I have to live with for the rest of my life. You are only as safe as the work ethics and morals of the health care provider and the mangers that run the venue.

The spa safety standards are still not as high as the restaurant safetyrequirements in the city. Spas try to squeeze in as many clients as they can in a day compromising the hygiene of the client and room. Just because the flyers look amazing and the decoration is amazing it is no indication of how clean the staff is. You will never be sure how safe you are in any massage environment, spa or resort and even a clinic.Your safest bet is to know the massage therapist and form a relationship with them making sure they do practice safety and proper hygiene by washing their hands before treatments and after they are done the massage.

The massage therapist is required by law to spray their massage table and use clean sheets. Look for the disinfectant table spray it should be somewhere in the massage room. Ask to see it. I find getting a mobile spa treatment one of your safest ways to insure cleanliness. If a therapist comes to your home you can see how they set up the table, if they are spraying it down and using clean sheets. Your massage therapist should tell you that they are going to wash their hands before touching you and wash their hands again if they have touched your feet and about to touch your face. In the last resort I worked in staff where wiping client's feet with hot towels and putting them back in the towel warmers afterwards. You can only imagine what type of bacteria was growing in some of these hot cabinets. You can only do so much and try to provide proper safety when the rest of your co-workers are not following the same standards as yourself. I can spray a massage table for my client but someone else might not do the same and the room is now compromised again. In the end you have to work in your own space at all times and control the sanitation and hygiene standards.

Hush

Hush now lonely one
The storm is gone
Mellow are the winds that pass
The sky's horizon reaches out
While summer breezes through
Your life is new
Today you meet your fate
You greet it with a kiss
Today is all there is
You make amends with winter's past
And worry not of what's to come
For it will come no matter what
It will come, to all and one
So savor all your sights and dreams
They come and go but never last
Set your sail and paddle on
Sail away for life goes on
Hush now lonely one
The storm is gone
Mellow are the winds that pass
The sky's horizon reaches out
While summer breezes through
Your life is new

CHAPTER THREE

Who Is Massaging You?

"When you come to the end of your rope tie a knot and hang on."
Franklin Roosevelt.

My next question for you is "Who do you allow to massage you?" After all it is your body and in my opinion if you are paying anywhere from eighty-five dollars and upto then you should make sure that the person working on you is a registered massage therapist with a license and proper training. First this assures you can get the coverage under your health benefits plan, and second you will have someone who can actually help you with any issues and answer your questions you might be experiencing physically. I have been in a couples massage room doing a treatment and for some reason the gentleman who was being massaged by an aesthetician did not have a clue that the massage was being performed by a non-massage therapist. He asked her questions about his knots and his back which she could not answer and was giving him short statements like "Yes you're tight there".

Many of you come into a spa completely ignorant that many of the times you are being passed on to an aesthetician and not given the proper information to make a decision on whether or not you want to be massaged by someone who is not trained like a massage therapist to work on your body. Those of you who are familiar with massage therapy and go to clinics or have a massage therapist that you see once a month or more frequently are more informed and would never risk getting a treatment from anyone but a professional especially when the price tag is in the high hundreds of dollars.

What is the difference between an aesthetician doing a massage or a registered massage therapist? The aesthetician goes to school to learn how to do aesthetics which covers waxing, make-up, pedicures, manicures, and some basic relaxation massage techniques. The bulk of their course is focused on skin care not massage therapy. Most of them do not have the proper ergonomics and stamina that the massage therapist has by having 2200 hours of just massage training and a wider science based study of body functions and illness. Many spas will use their aesthetician to perform a massage and charge the same as a registered massage therapy massage but pay the aesthetician lower wages. This is a big money saver for these spas and resorts but at the expense of the client. If the client happens to be very knowledgeable on massage therapy they will know when the hands that are touching them are professional or not. Most of these clients ask specifically for a registered massage therapist when booking the appointment to ensure they do receive the health benefits as well as the relaxation aspect of their treatment.

Some resorts I have worked in were very honest in telling the clients that they will not guarantee that the massage will be performed by a licensed massage therapist, others were misleading the public and just asking over the phone if they would need an insurance receipt or not? I have sat in the staff room waiting for a massage to come my way in this establishment while the aesthetician did most of the massage treatments and I was not being paid an hourly rate. I lost hundreds of dollars in wages day in and out watching aesthetician take over the massage portion of services. Some doing pregnancy treatments with no idea of how to perform it or make the mother to be safe?

Overall I did at times encounter spas and resorts that only allowed massage therapy to go to the registered massage therapists and aesthetics was reserved for the aesthetician only. This is in my opinion the best way to ensure you have a higher rate of satisfied clients that keep coming back for massage treatments. These spas know that in order to keep a good reputation especially in a city that has so much competition it is wise to only have the best service and professionals do what they were trained to do. Sadly I have also seen massage therapists cross the line and perform facials when they do not have training either. This puts the client at a high risk for skin damage and injury. Basically no one has the right to do a job that they are not trained to do or state thatthey are a massage therapist when they are not registered or trained. It is completely illegal and has severe penalties financial penalties. As a client if an aesthetician injures you during a treatment there is no governing body like the CMTO where you can file a complaint and this places you in a compromising situation. The qualifications of a trained massage therapy go beyond a relaxation massage and beauty. They are trained to asses you and help you with a fitness plan if required.

The CMTO is a body that helps protects the public against the malpractice of registered massage therapists. But who is protecting you against the greed and malpractice of spas that do not care if you are injured and allow professionals to perform a treatment on you that they are not able to do or trained for? I had the unfortunate experience of working in spas where they constantly booked me hot stone massages when I had no training for it. I was often told to take a video home with me and start doing hot stones on clients the next day. I simply refused and knew that I needed proper training in order to perform a hot stone massage safely and properly. The end results of not having such training as I have witnessed in places I have worked in is burnt marks on the clients back and law suits. These spas always have a help wanted sign online and are constantly replacing staff costing them money in training and a high turnover rate. Would it not be easier to just pay your registered massage therapist a good wage, only give massage treatments to the massage therapist and making sure that their training is top notch saving yourself the hassle of having to show up in court for causing injuries to your clients?

Be aware that when you are booking your massage in a spa or resort in Canada you might be getting an aesthetician, a registered massage therapist or someone who took a quick aromatherapy course? Remember that even if you do book with a registered massage therapist you might be disappointed because not every massage therapist is created equal. Some are excellent and have incredible hands and knowledge and others are better off looking for an alternative career because they simply were never meant to be a massage therapist. If you go to a clinic, a gym, or a wellness center you will only be receiving a massage by a registered massage therapist. Again your best choice is to build a long term relationship with your massage therapist to ensure proper care. Many spas and resort burn their massage therapists out and have a high turnover rate which leaves you starting over and losing contact with your massage therapist.

We have seen massage therapy on an incline in the past two decades but sometimes the cookie cutter spas and institution that want to benefit from financial rewards by offering these services do not have a clue about the operational aspects of having registered massage offered to their clients. They are blinded by dollar signs and do not have anyone's best interest at heart. We see massage being offered in hair salons, nail places, anywhere a chair can fit a sign will go up offering massage therapy. There are very strict laws and regulations that go hand in hand with performing massage therapy. Many of these owners do not know who the CMTO is and what they represent. So how can you run a massage business if you do not even know what a health history form looks like? I have been on interviews where the owners had no clue on the logistics of running a spa, massage therapy, or what it all entailed. To all these boutique owners, hair salons, and nail places, or sun tanning venues I have to tell you just focus on what you know and specialize in. Do not try to be all things to all people. A simple menu is best just like in the restaurant business the client needs to know what you specialize in and not be overwhelmed by too many choices. Less is more.

A safe environment in massage therapy means making sure the place is clean, only registered massage therapists are doing massages, and they are being paid fifty dollars and up for their services. We need to start rewarding our healers with a proper work environment and pay. This also means a break between treatments of thirty minutes if not more in order to give the therapist time to prepare themselves for their next client and clean the room and equipment.

This is where the government and the CMTO need to step in and insure that all spas, resorts, clinics, are hygienic and see that the bookings between clients are over five minutes, that the massage therapist has adequate time to eat, write notes, change the room properly, is paid according to their training, is not being burnt out and exploited which makes the client automatically walk into a safer environment. Massage therapists have to join forces and agree on what is acceptable and what needs to change to ensure these standards are being established. We should all be asking these questions. "Should we allow the aesthetician to perform massages and should it be part of their schooling?" or "Do we allow registered massage therapists to work in spas and resorts?" If we no longer have massage therapy covered under health insurance in the spa industry because it is considered leisure and not a health issue than massages in spas would typically only be performed by aesthetician.

What most spas count on is our license numbers and they make millions of dollars using our registration that costs us over seven hundred dollars a year to obtain. How do we change the law so that massage therapy is recognized as a medical career and not just a fluffy treatment for leisure and relaxation in the spa world? Who is looking after the registered massage therapist and making their profession an enjoyable experience and lucrative and respectable one as well?

Massage therapy is not well defined as of yet and maybe we should be looking for a different definition and naming it something entirely different leaving out the word massage out of the equation?raising our standards when it comes to training making it a four year degree in a University environment.

Aesthetics can remain focusing on skin care and beauty and that is when a one year course for spa massage can be established and a three to four year degree for the serious registered therapist who actually works in a clinical setting helping with car accidents and rehabilitation and athletes.

What I have learned in my five years practicing as a registered massage therapist is that the spa environment is not utilizing the skills learned in massage school to the fullest if at all. In a spa massage therapists are not being taken seriously has a health care provider. On average spas in Toronto and inCanada can pay their registered massage therapist anywhere from ten to twenty-three dollars an hour. It is a place that exploits the massage therapist, and for the most part does notrespect the professional or recognize the physical demand required to perform an hour massage on a client. If it did the practice of booking seven or more massages in a row with no breaks would not exist. Yet take a look at the bookings of spas across the province and see for yourself what a massage therapist schedules looks like and what they are subjected too.

In the summer of 2011 I had worked in my last spa or resort environment and knew that I was far too valuable in my willingness to help others and in my knowledge and abilities to keep myself in these environments that keep lowering my self-esteem and burning me out physically, and mentally. I wanted a proper work environment that was clean, healed, and paid me a living wage. I needed to have full control of what and how massage therapy was going to be performed putting the client's well-being first. It was all in my hands and being my own boss was the only way I could accomplish that.

At the very beginning of my career I believed in my heart that I was going to walk into favorable work places with a financial future that was going to be sound and abundant. I also believed that I was going to make a difference in the lives of the people I treated and came into contact with. In school we had guest speakers that advised us that the hotels and spas where some of the top paying jobs and best places to work in. But that never happened. In fact it was the opposite.

What I found in these places were bad management, poor wages, corruption, lack of health history forms, competition amongst massage therapist, jealousy, greed, and poor hygiene and aesthetics. I felt like an immigrant worker that was tied up to a sewing machine making one hundred dollar t-shirts for twenty cents an hour and not having a break or permission to choose how many clients I massaged in one day. Suddenly I understood what these workers were going through and I could relate to poverty and being overworked. It caused me several body injuries and no medical coverage to heal myself. I think you get the picture and the drama behind the scene in the spa industry is a great place for a writer to get material for a sitcom.

Walking past the waterfalls, the candles, the soft music, and the statue of the Buddha is a world of toxicity, and negative energy. Twenty-two spas and resorts in my five years and all of these places had taken advantage of me in one form or another forcing me many times to file complaints with owners, the CMTO, the labor board, and even the authorities. I have a folder filled with complaints to the CMTO, some to lawyers and the labor board trying to get justice on my side with no success while the exploitation keeps happening.

Do all registered massage therapists have the same experience as myself? Many of them do as I have watched my colleagues and former school mates go through the same experiences in some of the same work places I have been in. Some leave, some stay, some do not mind a wage of thirty-three dollars or even forty dollars for their work? Everyone is different and everyone's boundaries are set at a different level. We all choose what is right for ourselves but the truth is that he massages therapy industry needs to be reform on a governmental level and more has to be done to inform the public about safety as well as the benefits of massage therapy.

I have to admit that there is no other profession out there that touches clients and heals like massage therapy does. It is not a career for everyone. You have to have compassion for others, good hands, be intuitive, caring, patient, and you also need to be business minded to succeed in massage therapy. Most massage therapists have a hard time finding stability in the work force going from one place to another only to find that they have changed location but not politics. Booking your massage therapist nine massages with only a five minute break between clients is extremely abusive but this is being done right now as I write these words on this page. The massage therapists who enjoy their work are in control of the environment and have strong boundaries. They enjoy healing but making a decent wage at the same time. They know that if they burn out they will no longer be able to help others and continue to do what they enjoy doing. They work from home or in a clinic that has higher standards and they have a connections and relationship with their clients. Find yourself a reliable caring registered massage therapist with high standards and strong work ethics and you will never be disappointed again.

Rainbow Song

Wind murmurs, it is time
Shades of grey in fields adrift
While heat sits in my blood like wine
Trees sway, sky weeps
Scent of land fills the air
The ground is tempered
Tamed by the tears of the earth
Dew drops fall under leaves
And flows beneath the soil in thirst
Flowers bend with blades of grass
As they wait so eagerly
For the coming of the sun
Whose very lips are trimmed with gold
The dusk sparkles with a faithful kiss
I will not meet the deadened hour
For my soul leaps in ecstacy
And unrestrained delight
In this magical affair
With color and light

CHAPTER FOUR

Sexual Harrassment and Massage Parlors

"They cannot take away our self-respect if we do not give it to them."
Mahatma Gandhi

I could not write about massage therapy without covering Sexual harassment and the old age profession of prostitution. We are all aware of massage parlors in the city and outside as well. We still confuse the world of massage therapy with the world of happy endings. This is due to the fact that in a city of Toronto for example there are over three thousand massage parlors that operate under the guise of holistic massage therapy. Therefore when someone who is not familiar with clinical massages performed by a registered massage therapist and sees the word "Massage" on a sign the automatic response that goes into the mind of these clients is the word "Sex." Massage and Sex become one in the same.

My school could never have prepared me for the world I was about to embark on as far as being sexually propositioned over the years. The topic of sexual harassment did not come up in class and in my opinion it should be a course and the student should really be made aware of how prevalent it really is. Not only did I have to endure the constant negative work environments that I had been subjectedto over the years but I also was being grabbed, exposed, and propositioned for sexual favors by ignorant clients. I also learned that this happened to most of my colleagues as well and that it happened more often that one thought for both male and female therapists. Sitting around at work and sharing our stories about being propositioned was sometimes quite humorous because everyone had a different way of handling the situation and frankly I really am amazed at what some people are capable of. For example grabbing a male therapist's ass in a couple's massage while his wife is lying beside him? Pick your gender if you may? Some therapists are forgiving and will give the client a second chance to redeem themselves but not everyone is that charitable.

A combination of bad publicity, with some massage therapists havingcrossed professional boundaries with clients in work places, anda lack of public awareness make sexual harassment a common denominator in the life of massage therapists. It did not matter if you worked in a clinic or a spa the potential for someone to ask for sexual favors or to expose them to you were real and happened too often. Almost everyone I knew from school, teachers, and co-workers had a sexual harassment story to tell including myself.

In my five years of being a massage therapists I have had twenty dollar bills waved at me as I entered a room to do a thirty minute massage, I have had men ask me where the showers where before their booked thirty minute massage, I had the pleasure of having a man expose his private parts three times while I massaged him and finally walked out of the room. We also received phone calls from clients asking if we did sexual massages. Besides having some intoxicated clients who could hardly walk to the massage room and then grab my arms during the treatment, I had the privilege of having chronic moaners who got themselves off by making orgasmic sounds for the entire hour youwere treating them. Recently I have had less of these experiences as I do not tolerate the above scenarios and will walk out of the room if I feel uncomfortable and will charge the full session.

If you walk into a professional massage place you will be asked to fill out a health history form. This is your first clue that it is not a massage sexual parlor. Look at how the massage therapists are dressed? That is your second clue. Are they wearing a bra and underwear or a polo shirt and gym pants? Most massage parlors have illegal immigrants from overseas as sex slaves working against their will performing sexual favors. Just because you see the word Massage on a business sign does not mean you are in a sex parlor.

Massage therapists are at a higher risk bracket when it comes to being exposed to sexual offenders and part of the reason is that the city of Toronto has three thousands if not more illegal sex parlors in operation. Secondly the media does nothing to inform the public about massage therapy and the benefits of massage and how it is used for improving health and wellness. Not too long ago we had scandals with politicians in massage parlors or massage therapists in the media who accused politicians of sexual harassment placing massagetherapy ina negative spotlight. The word *massage* alone connotes sex in the minds of too many people and is made fun of on television shows and sitcoms which furthers the misinterpretation of the profession giving it a bad reputation. It reminds me of a Sinefield episode when George received a massage from a male therapist because the female therapist was with Elaine. When he became aroused during the treatment he questioned his sexuality.

A mobile massage business can become dangerous for the massage therapist if she or he does not have a way of keeping safe before going into someone's home without prior knowledge of who the person is. Some spas also make the massage therapist work in client's hotel room. Again this is risky business without a back-up plan. You never know whose room you're walking into. The risk is always there and without a way out if you need help it could be your last time you perform a massage on someone. I do not condone massage parlors and the fact that we are all being placed under the same umbrella is often times discouraging.

A registered massage therapist is a health care provider and not a prostitute. We need stricter laws that protect massage therapists against sexual predators by the spa owners, and the law in general. If you know that the sexual advances on a massage therapist in a professional environment can cost you some serious consequences or a fine, time in court, and embarrassment than you would think twice about doing it in the first place. You do not make advances when you are at your doctor's office so bear in mind that the same boundaries should be in place with your massage therapist.

I know that it is the only profession out there that requires you as a client to take your clothes off, but you are covered at all times and proper draping was established by the profession for this reason. I have had clients in the past tell me that there was too much fuss over the draping and sheets. Some of these clients like to expose themselves by taking off their robes in front of the massage therapist or lying on top of the massage bed in the nude and not under the covers.

Massage and sex are not one in the same. Many female clients are reluctant to have a male therapist work on them. Again you have a right to choose who is doing your massage and if a female makes you feel safer for any reason then you have every right to ask for one. But because I am a massage therapist I know that sex is the last thing on a therapist's mind for the most part. There are exceptions to the rules and that is true in any profession. But a male therapist is stronger usually and I will choose a massage therapist based on how good they are and not on gender. They are not judging your body, how skinny or fat you are. School really engraves ethics and professionalism in our minds for two years and before we head out into the work force we are fully trained to treat the client and nothing more.

We have a long way to go before we can erase the sexual connotations associated with massage therapy but I believe that the day will arrive in the next decade or so. We will value massage therapy for what it is a healing art, science and much more. It is every massage therapist's obligation to educate their clients, and not make fun of the profession by supporting to stop any sexual harassment that takes place at work, and educate the public on this issue along with the media, and government. It is also important for you out there to speak up and file a complaint with the CMTO if you have been the victim at the hands of a massage therapist who has crossed the line and touched you in an unprofessional manner. We do not have room in the profession for unprofessional therapists who make our reputation a bad one and lower our standards as a whole. Sexual favors are not covered under your health insurance and sex has no place in the life of a professional massage therapist. All the jokes, the humor that people put out there when it comes to massage therapy are in poor taste and do not belong in our professional life. Your massage therapist has spent two years of their lives if not more to help you heal and recover from an injury, help you with child birth, assisted you with you dying parents, and family members, massaged your children, in a way that no other health care provider has. We are one of the few professions left that listen to clients and touch them. Do you know how many people out there need this kind of support in their lives? Let us all be mindful of what massage therapy really is and what it is not by giving it the respect it deserves. Let's take the Sex out of Massage.

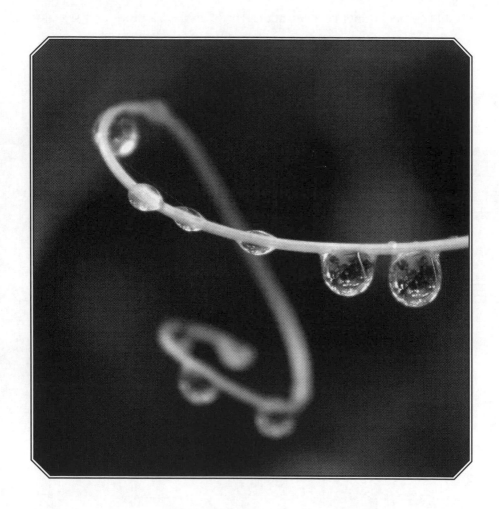

Beautiful Things

I find myself drawn
To beautiful things
Now more than ever
They are the simplest things too
All my little joys
My new found pleasures
Slowly emerging
Like a hidden flower
Blooming in my Soul

CHAPTER FIVE

The Benefits of Massage Therapy

"If you understand the force of
intelligence in the body, its mechanical
operation and structure, you can work
on any part of the body you can reach
with your hands."

Lauren Berry

So what is massage therapy really about? What are the benefits and its effects on the body?" Why do so many insurance and health benefits cover it? First let's understand an important fact. All massage schools in Canada teach Swedish massage. I do not want you to get confused with the term that you see being used in spas like holistic or deep tissue. These words have no real meaning and are there to mislead you into paying for something that is Swedish based. Deep tissue is a Swedish massage with more pressure in the spa world. The word holistic has no meaning in the world of massage. What is the definition of holistic? This is a word that is over used with no meaning or place in massage therapy. It could mean that you are getting an aesthetician instead of a registered massage therapist to do your treatment and nothing more. Holistic by definition means dealing with the whole person and the entire being. His/ her physical, emotional, spiritual, mental, and social environmental factors. Does that seem like a massage treatment that is remotely possible by anyone's standards?

Massage Therapy is the manipulation of superficial and deeper layers of muscle and connective tissue. It helps with the healing process and is also used for relaxation or reduces stress. The word massage is French meaning friction or kneading. In massage the therapist manipulates the body with pressure manually or with mechanical aids. Tissues being worked on are muscles, tendons, ligaments, fascia, skin, and joints to name a few. Therapists can use hands, fingers, elbows, forearms, knees or feet to apply pressure and massage their clients.

Massage therapy increases blood circulation and helps rid the body of toxins that are built up in the body. It can also help recovery time for athletes after a sport event or working out in the gym. The reason for choosing massage therapy can range from relaxation and decreasing stress, to dealing with injuries or a chronic health condition. The use of massage therapy as a therapeutic health benefit dates back four thousand years in Chinese medicine. Here in America massage dates back since 1850 and by the end of the 19th century doctors where practicing it. When technology and prescription drugs came about massage disappeared for a long time until the seventies and made a comeback.

Today massage therapy is highly in demand with the increase of computer work and the seeking of alternative medicine by the general public for improving health. I have gathered a list of different massages that you will often see being offered in different venues. Not all of these techniques are performed by registered massage therapists. Some therapists choose to add it to their continuing education and others massage techniques are performed by a student who took a course in the different type of body work.

Swedish Massage

Swedish massage uses long flowing strokes known as effleurage, petrissage, tapotment, friction, vibration or shaking. It helps in reduction of pain, joint stiffness, and increase circulation. The Dutch practitioner Johan Georg Mezger adopted the French names to label the basic strokes.

Aromatherapy Massage

A real aromatherapy massage is performed by someone who might not be registered but has a knowledge base on essential oils and its effect on the individual. There are hundreds of essential oils with different properties and health benefits. Adding a few drops of essential oils in a bottle of massage oil is not an aromatherapy massage. It takes months of study to know all the plants and flower based or herbs used in making essential oils. Pregnant clients are not recommended to use these as it may harm the fetus.

Cranial-Sacral Massage

This massage uses very gentle pressure and is applied to the head and spine to correct imbalances and restore the flow of cerebrospinal fluid. A massage therapist might want to take additional training and add this form of massage to help clients with different conditions. They have studies that help with ADD and head injuries for example.

Lymphatic Massage

This is a light and rhythmic technique used to help improve the flow of the lymph fluid. This is a liquid that is in the body to help fight infection and disease. When these nodes are compromised there is an inflammation of the legs or area and massage will help regain normal function.

Myofascial Release

With the gentle pressure and body positioning the body relaxes, and the muscle is stretched then the fascia which is a connective tissue is also affected and the related structures.

Reflexology

This is a course taken by massage therapists or non-therapists. It is a technique that focuses on the hands and feet. It is believed that the areas have reflex points and direct connections to specific organs and structure throughout the body.

Rolfing

Deep pressure is applied to the fascia to stretch it, and lengthen it so it can become more flexible. The technique helps with realignment of the body releasing tension.

Shiatsu

Using gentle finger and hand pressure the therapist uses specific points on the body, to relieve pain and enhance the flow of energy pathways that are called meridians. It is based on the oriental massage techniques.

Bowen Therapy

Bowen technique involves a rolling of movements over fascia, muscle, ligaments, tendons, and joints. It is not a deep massage with a long contact with muscle tissue like most massages but does restore muscle tensions, strains, and normal lymphatic flow. This type of massage is very gentle it can be done on newborn babies or the elderly. Tom Bowen a native of Australia developed the technique and passed it along all over the world.

Deep Tissue Massage

this type of massage is used to relief severe tension in the muscle and the connective tissue or fascia (A fascia is a <u>connective tissue</u> that surrounds muscles, groups of muscles, blood vessels, and nerves, binding those structures together in much the same manner as <u>plastic wrap</u> can be used to hold the contents of sandwiches together.[2] It consists of several layers: a superficial fascia, a deep fascia, and a subserous (or visceral) fascia and extends uninterrupted from the head to the tip of the toes.[3]

This type of massage focuses on muscle located below the surface of the top muscles. It is great on clients that have chronic pain, who are athletic, or are injured. It is common to feel ache for two days after a deep tissue massage. The term "Deep Tissue" is misused to identify a massage that is performed with deep pressure throughout the entire session. Deep tissue massage is used to work on a particular set of muscles that the client complains about by using a set of techniques to help relieve aches or pains. It is NOT a deep pressure massage. Deep tissue is applied to superficial and deep layers of muscles and fascia or other structures and can be very intense. It would be impossible to give a deep tissue massage for an hour without causing injury to localized muscles and nerves.

Sport Massage

Often used by professional athletes to treat sports related injuries. It enhances performance and helps with recovery time. In order for a registered massage therapist to practice sports massage an additional set of hours must be taught at a sport clinic.

Trigger Point Massage

Pressure is applied to tender knotted areas in the body. This helps dissolve the knots and release pain and tension. It can be used to help with muscle spasms. This technique is painful but very helpful. Sometimes this type of massage is confused with pressure point massage. Trigger points cause local pain or refer pain such as headaches in other parts of the body. Janet G Travell and David Simons discovered and mapped out trigger points in the body.

Hot Stone Massage

Using stones usually basalt stones that retain heat and releases it rapidly the stones are used in the treatment as an extension of the therapist's hands using them as a tool. The stones are also placed on the body in energy centers. This can be performed in spas by a registered massage therapist or an aesthetician. Personally I do not enjoy performing a hot stone massage and find it to be a new trend that will lose its hype eventually.

Reiki

With reiki you do not need to be a massage therapist to learn body energy work. The person performing reiki does not touch the body of the client for the most part. They are working with chakras and energy centers to unblock past lives help with negative energy. Reiki was developed by a Buddhist monk called Mikao in 1922. Reiki is the transfer of ki energy to the client through the palms and has many levels of apprenticeship until one becomes a Reiki master.

Prenatal and Antenatal Massage

This is given to women during their pregnancy by a trained massage therapist whotakes additional courses after graduating from massage school. We do cover pregnancy massage in school but further education is needed to become well versed in all stages of pregnancy and the effects of massage on the mother and unborn child. This type of massage use to be done by midwives to help before and after pregnancy.

Thai Massage

This is one type of massage that I studied in school as one of my electives and after I graduated. There are many levels in Thai massage. The client is fully clothed in comfortable gym clothes. They are placed on a mat on the floor while the therapist starts rhythmic strokes and then stretches the muscles into different poses while also using Shiatsu pressure point techniques. This is very effective for relaxation and muscle tension relief.

Active Release Techniques

This was developed and used mostly by chiropractors but many registered massage therapists use it to treat injuries, mostly for scar tissue, adhesions, and nerve compressions.

Lomilomi

This is a Hawaiian massage. It is indigenous and varies by island or family. The practitioner uses forearms, finger, knuckles, feet, sticks and stones to perform the massage but technique vary from one therapist to another. The word lomilomi is used for massage in Soma and East Futuna.

Tuina massage

is a Chinese based massage treatment. It is a form of Chinese manipulative therapy used in conjunction with acupuncture, mosxibustion, and fire cupping, herbalism, tai chi and qigong. It also uses Taoist principals as well as martial arts.

These types of massage are the ones you are most likely to encounter on a spa menu or some clinics or wellness centers. A registered massage therapist will continue to educate themselves on different types of massages and adding courses and workshops throughout their years in practice. A massage therapist is only as good as their dedication to continuing education, and adding courses and knowledge to their Swedish base education. In a clinical setting with a very proficient massage therapist one can regain range of motion, and help heal injuries and regain balance into one's life. A clinical assessment is a great tool to help you aware of where you stand in you injury and also helps the therapist write a proper long or short term plan.

Massage therapy is practiced internationally and Canada alongside with France which requires three years of practice and Germany has a very high standard for massage therapy professionals. In Canada only the three provinces which are British Columbia, Ontario, and Newfoundland and Labrador are regulated. Other countries have different requirements for becoming a therapist. For example in South Korea only the blind and visually impaired can become licensed masseurs. In Mexico therapists are called sob adores, a form of faith healing and acupuncture. In the United States there are about three hundred thousand license massage therapists every state differs in the requirements for the license and practice of massage, in 1997 one hundred and fourteen million people went to see a massage therapist in the US. It is one of the most used alternative medicines in that country.

Keep in mind this information next time you decide to head out to a spa or resort outside of Canada or another province that is not registered. You might be putting yourself in harm's way with no back up if something happens to you or you get injured and I have seen it happen several times in the last five years. Always be mindful of who is treating you and what their qualifications are. Not all massage therapists are created equally across the lines, boundaries, nations, and countries. But I hope to have at least made some of the types of massages that you have encountered along the way well defined and remember not to get sucked into a gimmick or something that has a fancy name with not real reward attached to it.

It takes time and years for a registered massage therapist to get very good at one specific technique. The two year program does not make us experts in all massage types and not all therapists want to focus on sports or deep tissue treatments. What the massage program does do is educate us in pathology and help us focus our treatments to help a client who has a medical condition. Every therapist is different on what they focus on with the two year sometimes three year course and what path they decide to embark upon. Which means that not all registered massage therapist will be able to help you if they haven't taken extra courses let's say for example for your TMJ problems, or a Deep Tissue focused treatment on a specific injury.

On A Canvas By The Sea

The sun sojourns briefly
I see them vaguely
Haunting images
Of history
On a canvas by the sea
Blending in with mists of today
With shades of grey
Dividing and uniting
Lost worlds
Lost voices
Of my roots
A sudden wave
Compels my soul
I hear the grace of tongues
From the other side
They have found me
And in this brief moment
Of parting mists
I am left with no choice
But to listen, and watch
As the dusk awakens the lakes
The veil is thin

CHAPTER SIX

The Do's and Don'ts... Proper Spa Ethics

"The difference between ordinary and
extraordinary is that little extra."

Jimmy Johnson

Before you head out to the spa or clinic or wellness center for your next massage here is some information I put together for you to make the process easy and a pleasant experience. Whether this is your first time getting a massage or you want to experience a day at the spa with your partner or friends the following will give you the DOs and DON'Ts of massage.

1. Find out who is going to be performing your massage. Who are you allowing to touch you for the hour or ninety minutes? Is the therapist registered? There is nothing more frustrating than paying good money to walk out of the spa disappointed and unsatisfied. Ask around from friends and family that have had a particular massage therapist and was pleased with the service and facility. Beware of spas or venues that use other massage therapist's license numbers and pretend that the therapist is an actual registered massage therapist. I have seen this happen to a colleague of mine who worked

in a chiropractic office. Her license number was being used after she was no longer there. Unless you like light massages I do not recommend having a treatment by an aesthetician either. In the United States aesthetician are not allowed to perform massage or advertise for them. I believe we should follow their example in Canada but unless we reform who is permitted to treat or not, then simply ask for a registered massage therapist before you book. If you get hurt during a massage you will be able to contact the CMTO to complain but with someone who is not registered you have nowhere to go and are left unprotected.

2. Make sure that the spa or place you are attending is clean. Check the locker rooms, bathrooms, and treatment rooms for signs of hairs or dirt. This is not always an indication that the tables are being wiped down with disinfection spray or that the sheets are not being layered or reused. I have seen five and four star resorts have a lack of hygiene so there is no way of telling if you are safe or not until wechange inspections laws.

3. Do not book a massage if you are ill or getting over a cold. You will be putting everyone at risk in the spa or clinic center you are attending. I once massaged a close friend who had the flu and I was sick the day after for a month with severe fever and sore throat unable to hear out of one ear. It was the worst mistake on my part thinking I was going to help her get over her misery faster only to cause my own. Many spas expect the therapist to treat regardless if they are sick or not. We all know that we are not allowed to go into work as a massage therapist when we have an illness or a cough. Be respectful and stay home until you are better.

4. Do not eat or drink alcohol before your treatment. This will affect your massage as you are digesting food and massage increases your blood circulation. Alcohol consumption can

be dangerous as the blood is diluted and the effects of the massage will make the client dizzier after the treatment is over. Also do not come hung over. Enjoy your session.

5. Come on time. If your appointment is at ten am you should be on the table and ready for your treatment at ten not ten o five. Come fifteen minutes early to fill out your health history form and do not assume that your therapist will be able to make up for your lateness. Most of the time there is someone else who will be getting a treatment right after you and cannot be left waiting. In most places you will be charged for the hour you booked and you will have your treatment time cut. But be aware of massage therapists who cut your time out of laziness. They do this by hiding the clock or putting something in front of it. Make sure you get your full hour.

6. Fill out your health history form fully. Do not leave your operations, surgeries, allergies, or anything else than can affect you during the massage. You would be surprised at how many people that do not disclose pertinent information that can put them at harm's way. A health history form is a legal document that protects both the therapist and the client.

7. Wear comfortable clothing and discuss with your therapist the areas you want to be worked on and the areas you do not want them to touch. Allow for proper attire for the massage of your areas that will be worked on. You are always under the sheets and no body parts will be exposed. Underwear on or off? It's up to you to decidewhat you are comfortable with.

8. Do not wear jewelry. Many times I have seen clients lose jewelry at the spa because they come in wearing necklaces, bracelets, and watches to the massage treatments. It is best to leave sentimental and expensive jewelry at home or back

in your hotel room. Besides it gets in the way of a proper massage.

9. Keep your robe on until the massage therapist has reviewed your health history form and communicated with you about what type of treatment they will be performing. No one wants to stand in front of someone who is naked.

10. Massage time is not a time to worry about your make-up smearing on the sheets or how you look afterwards, if you have no plans after your treatments and you are not worried about oil in your hair or face you will have a fantastic experience.

11. Do not leave your flip flops and shoes or boots around the massage table where the therapist can trip or fall. There is always a designated area for your clothes and articles so that the massage therapist can work safely and allows you not to have your clothing on the floor.

12. Beware of gimmicks. Spas are famous for creating ways to make you spend money on a treatment that should be the same cost as an hour Swedish massage. Deep tissue, aromatherapy, are examples of ways to increase the price for a treatment when in reality it is just an adjustment of pressure and for aromatherapy a nice smelly oil that will add anywhere from five to ten dollars for your treatment. Also the ionic foot bath is not scientifically proven to help you with any weight loss of other issues. It is also not covered under your insurance policy and should not be put through by the spa or clinic as such. Save your money for what you came in for.

13. If you are pregnant ask your doctor if it is safe for you to have a massage. Some women are at high risk for miscarriages and massage is not a good idea especially at the first trimesters of pregnancy.

14. Take a shower before your massage. I have had the unfortunate times of having clients with severe body odor that made me wonder if I was going to make it through the hour. It makes

the massage therapist not able to focus properly or want to give you a proper treatment when they are uncomfortable. If you are having a foot massage wash your feet and make sure you are wearing deodorant. This means check your breath for onion or garlic breath too. The massage therapist should also be aware of their body odor and bad breath.

15. Do not make out with your partner in the lobby or waiting room. If you are laughing right now at this statement believe me I have seen it happen many times. Staff and front desk personnel can see you and often there are cameras looking right at you. You are risking the embarrassment of being kicked out of the facility and this lacks respect for other guests that are trying to enjoy their day as well without having to feel like they are in a parlor instead of a spa.

16. Leave your cell phone in your locker, or simply turn it off. I have experience clients who wasted thirty minutes of their treatment talking on their cell phones or have left them ringing the entire hour. You are here to relax. Leave the office behind for that one hour.

17. Do not take a shower if there is one in the room unless you have cleared it with front desk upon reservation. Remember there is someone else right after you and the room needs to be cleaned.

Do your research and ask a lot of questions before booking your next spa or massage appointment to minimize disappointment. The best time to go for a massage is when you can rest after the treatment. Unfortunately many spas and resorts will make you leave the massage room right after without any extra pampering or place to lounge and take in the work that was done on you.

Make sure you drink plenty of water after a massage. This is important to help release any toxins that were released into circulation and re-hydrate you. If you can go home and relax further after a treatment and not have any plans I believe this can be the best way to enjoy the benefits of a great massage. Try not to have any distraction afterwards, or go to the gym. This is "Me" time and my advice to you is to make a day of it.

Resonance

Remnants of time past
They know not where to go
Trapped and hidden
In the chambers
Of a lost Soul
What is there to do
But to orchestrate
This moment?
All that is left
All the pieces and truths
Into a symphony of Love
Where melody and song
Fills the room
With resonance

CHAPTER SEVEN

Our Path Into Wellness

"Take care of your body, it's the only
place you have to live."

Jim Rohn

We live in a very unique time. Our environment, water supply, obesity rate, and the way we do business affect our everyday lives and our future. We are in a very delicate balance and most of us feel the tension and worries that we all face as a whole like no other time in history. As you can see when greed and making a buck comes before the wellbeing of humanity we see the ripple effects it has on everyone and everything.

The obesity rate in youngsters and adults is now an epidemic which was something unheard of when I was a child growing up. What has changed? We now have a generation of children that do not know where food comes from. They have never seen a vegetable be planted or grow. The food that they consume comes out of a box and put in a plastic container in the microwave.

Cancer and illness is on the rise. We have created a world of convenience and are now seeing the devastating effects and consequences of our laziness, and greedy cooperate world that has raped the earth, destroyed its habitat and we are lost in the balance of try to make it all better. How much money does one person need to be happy? Can we not leave it alone and still do business?

The media is constantly throwing out messages about beauty, and reality television brain washes our youth into a world that is shallow and plastic. We are in a crisis morally, financially, and environmentally.

But let me focus on the topic of wellness because this is what I do for a living and this is what I am passionate about in my professional life. My own beliefs are based on intuition and that we are more than just a body but that we also have a higher self. There are no accidents and we all have our reasons for being born and having this human experience. We do not fully understand the human potential and science alone does not have all the answers. We are aware that the human mind is powerful in creating the life that we experience. The law of attraction has been a hot topic for the last five years with books like The Secret.

What makes each of us decide how we are going to act today?

Why be responsible and kind and caring?

Is it because someone else told you this is what you must do?

We all have a responsibility in creating the world we live in. Individually I believe we all want to achieve success in work, family, and health. But many of us fall short in one or all of those areas.

Without action nothing in our lives changes for the better. You have to really want to make those changes and take action in order to see results. There is no magic pill or quick solutions to anyone's health issues or work and relationship problems. Become aware of yourself and see how your actions today affect your future.

There are alternative ways of healing the body besides prescription drugs and massage therapy is one of those alternative choices that one can make in improving their health. Like any health care alternative massage therapy also has its limits on what it can achieve in recovery. In order to achieve a body that is agile and has less pain you have to be willing to take responsibility for your health. This means watching what you eat, working out regularly with no excuses of not having time or money.

Nutrition is instrumental to a healthy body. It affects your muscle and body systems in a way that you do not realize. When you feed your body the wrong foods, you will be breaking down the machine and aging prematurely eventually causing dysfunction to set in and disease. Add smoking, drugs or alcohol consumption and you are in for a complete breakdown and body pain. Eat real food as much as you can. It is actually easier to peel a banana or eat an apple than throwing a TV diner in the microwave. Your body needs to be fed on a cellular level to balance out blood sugar. When your liver and kidneys are over burden by poor diet and sugar laced foods and alcohol consumption it stops metabolizing fats and eventually breaks down

I can feel with my hands the condition my client's body is in by the texture of muscle tissue, knots, tension, muscle tone, and whether they are hydrated or not. Someone who sits at a desk all day and consumes processed foods all the time and does not work out has a body composition or muscle tone that is weak. You do not need to be an athlete to be in good shape but you must eat properly and make exercise part of your life. Being sedentary and booking a massage every month will not help you reach long term health benefits.

After food choices I will place exercise in the top ten lists of health and well-being. Many of you come to see me with low back pain, sciatic nerve impediments, and other complaints. In most cases this is happening to clients that do not workout, have poor posture, work at a desk all day, and have poor core strength or muscle tone. Exercise has to become part of your lifestyle without even batting an eyelid. Make it fun and part of your daily routine. Even if you decide to go for walks every day you will be on your way to improving your health. Muscles that are tight and weak do not have proper blood flow which causes chronic knots and pain. We are not built to be sitting at a desk all day for hours. Our bodies are designed for movement.

We rehabilitate injuries and accidents by making the patients or clients move as fast as possible. Gone are the days where bed rest was prescribed or neck braces. The muscles need blood and nutrients to have recovery. I see my clients with sciatica because they areoverweight and you are not working out at all. They sit in a chair all day and their stomach muscles are flabby. No wonder their low back hurts. But this is the reason why most of the time my clients have issues. The massage therapist is limited in what they can do to relieve this tension if the client does not take part in their own recovery taking home the remedial exercise given to them after the treatment. Massage therapy is not a magic pill.

Stress is the number one cause of illness and I am exposed to clients that have stressful lives at work and at home. There seems to be less time for leisure and more time spent at the office. Add the daily chores and pressure ofraising a family or sometimes the care taking of the elderly for some of my clients. This type of stress takes its toll on the health of my clients and massage will give them a break from thinking about their careers, work or family. We all have stress in our lives and deadlines. Besides massage I suggest you try meditation as well and take a few moments each day to be alone and turn your mind off. Try to practice living in the now not in the past or the future. Surround yourself with supportive and positive friends and let the negative ones go. Create the environment you want for yourself and do something nice or relaxing every day.

Cleansing is also something that I do on a regular basis. It helps my body get rid of toxins from the environment and release fats out of my body. I have acleanse that I use and a nutritional program that has helped me maintain my weight and wellness. Let your digestive track relax for a day by not eating any food. You will feel more energy. I have seen improved health with my skin, hair, nails, sleep patterns, and energy levels with cleansing.

I also like using virgin organic coconut oil internally and externally. It has many health benefits like an anti-bacterial, weight loss, and I use it to moisturize my body and hair. Coconut oil is a good source of saturated fat. The principal fatty acid is lauric acid also found in human breast milk. It is an antiviral, antimicrobial which also helps with our immune system and making it stronger. If you suffer from heartburn coconut oil will help the digestive track and irritable bowel syndrome. Coconut has been used to fight against herpes, AIDS, and candida. The properties of coconut oil are endless.

Give back to your community in one way or another. This can be in a form of community service or giving a donation to a charity of your choice. There are hundreds of causes to donate time or money to. You will be reaching out to the people in your community and making a difference in the lives of others. Not everyone is fortunate enough to have a loving home or family, a safe place to live, food or shelter. If you were blessed this year with all of the above than giving some of your time is a way to give thanks for what you do have.

I believe that doing business in an ethical manner saves you money and time in the long run. When your massages therapists are treated well, paid a good wage, are not being burnt out they will be given the tools to give excellent service. Kindness has its rewards. There is no need for egotistical management styles it only makes a corporation and a place of business weak and loses potential customers down the line. The owners and professionals that go the extra mile in making your experience a safe one and enjoyable will also enjoy the success and rewards and most of all satisfaction going above the standards of most places I have worked in. When you help others succeed you also make yourself grown and become more successful. The law of abundance cannot be cheated sooner or later what goes around will come around.

A sound spa and clinic or wellness center has happy well paid staff. For a registered massage therapist this means they are being compensated for sitting around waiting for a walk in and not being taken for granted. When they are performing a treatment they are being paid well. They also have sufficient down time between clients to write notes and clean the room properly. They are allowed to sit and eat a proper meal in a proper staff room. Managers and owners are hands on and listen to the concerns of their staff and commit to monthly staff meetings. There is no favoritism and everyone has a fair amount of treatments book but the massage therapist has the last word about how many treatments they are able to do without the fear of losing their job when they are booked nine and eight treatments. Everyone sticks to their expertise and there is no lines being crossed professionally. Your therapist does not promise you a treatment that they are not able to do. This is the type of environment you want to spend time in and money. The energy is positive and the care you will receive in this center is top notch. You are able to relax further after you massage and you are given remedial exercise and advice afterwards. In this spa or resort you are not cattle being herded from one room to the next.

We do not need more fast food chains in massage therapy being created where no one really benefits except the franchise itself. If you are conscious of the environment, the food you eat, what you buy and support then think twice before you head out to your next spa venture or resort? You might me supporting business practices that you disagree with. The wellness centers and retreats are a great place to get treated in a way that focuses on the individual's health care needs. Nutritionists, Chiropractors, Life Couches, and Personal Trainers make an excellent team along with Yoga Teachers, and Meditation Centers. Look for a retreat or wellness center that does not focus on beauty but makes wellness their focal point. Also look for a place that is conscious about the environment and is practicing green procedures by using organic products and recycling.

Bring The Voice

Bring the Light
Bring the rain
Night of Soul
Hour of pain
Bring the Voice
Bring it all
Let your song
Break the wall

CHAPTER EIGHT

The Good and Ugly

"If you can find a path with
no obstacles. it probably doesn't
lead anywhere."

Frank A.Clark

They say that everything happens for a reason and when I look back at the last fifteen years of my life I realize that everyone I have met the good and the bad, has lead me in some way on the path to becoming a massage therapist.Along the way I learned what was acceptable for me and what was not. I see my car accident in 1994 as a blessing. It led me into the arms of an exceptional massage therapist who taught me the art of healing. I also look back now at all of the twenty-two spas, resorts, and clinics for teaching me through their injustice why it is important to have high standards to begin with.

Self-esteem was a factor and so was facing my fears of the unknown. Once I embraced these lessons I realized that I could go through the process of building my own massage business with the ethics and standards that was lacking in my previous work places. Inorder to become a better health care provider I had to be happy and fit but also able to survive finically. This book would not exist without having had contact with each and every individual that made my life hard at times and made me want to quit the profession. They too were excellent teachers and healer. There is no harm done that no good can come out of. The people that make our lives the hardest are indeed are greatest teachers. In hardship there is a place for growth and development.

The clients that I have also come into contact with over the years have helped me make this book a reality. Through the care and touch of their bodies I was able to learn about health, and how each person is so unique in the way that they perceive life and view the world in general. Many of my client's stories and experiences have stayed with me to this day. I have helped some of them recover fully from accidents, put a smile on their faces during a session. I have shared my health and nutritional view with some of them. Only in this profession have I had people come up to me with complements and appreciation for what I do for a living. I have shared the birth of a child and massaged the mother to be the night before giving them comfort and hope. I have helped clients start a fitness program and watch them a few years later achieve outstanding physical performance by re-shaping their physic. Some have joined local yoga classes and quit their jobs to later become yoga teachers. My words and support has had long term effects on the lives of my clients and no other profession quit compares to having this type of positive impact in the lives of people. A massage therapist can uplift, relieve pain, give support, and help in times of massive crisis like 911. The list is endless when the focus and intent of the therapist is pure and honest.

There are so many positive stories that were created over the course of my five years in the profession. I thank all of the clients that have allowed me to touch them and share with them my knowledge and experience in wellness. They are all my reason of being who I am today. Without them I would not have enjoyed the journey as a registered massage therapist. When someone trusts you to care for them and trust that you will help them get better it is one of the greatest honors and I never take that for granted. My clients are my reason for writing this book as well as my thirst for guiding all of you into a world of massage whether it is your first time or you are well seasoned massage goer.

As a consumer you have many options to choose from. You have every right to choose your therapist, how much pressure you want and where. You have the right to have a safe and clean facility that does not manipulate you into a gimmick or not give you all the facts. If any place out there should be spiritual and sacred it is a massage therapy place and spa. The future of the profession lies with all of us. From the consumer who pays for the treatment to the massage therapist and setting higher standards as a whole to the CMTO and government for making more legislations and improving the work force. Without these changes the future of massage therapy will be bleak and remain a very unsatisfying professional choice that will leave its student disappointed. What kind of changes would you like to see in the massage therapy profession? What kind of experiences have you had in a spa or clinical setting? Is there a massage therapist that has touched you and healed you in a way that you never thought would be possible?

Everything in life takes time and effort to change. Massage therapy has come a long way in the last twenty years but needs to change in the next two decades in a way that it will be main stream and accepted as a real health benefit by the public. It also needs to be set apart from the world of aesthetics, and prostitution when the price and time of schooling is so high and the upkeep of licensing is also expensive. These worlds can no longer collide and massage therapy needs more exposure in the media by athletes who benefit as a result of being exposed to it as well as making massage a permanent place in health care such as hospitals, and clinics.

From a very young age my life has revolved around wellness whether I was aware of it or not. At the age of five I was taking ballet classes and excelled at it. In school I enjoyed gymnastics and any form of sports like baseball, basketball, or soccer. At age of sixteen I was a regular at local gym weight training and became a vegetarian for the next twenty years of my life. When I did introduce meat again to my diet it had to be organic and I needed to know the source of its origin. I have cleansed since my teen years, worked out, meditated, and made food and exercise a focal point in my life. Although I believe we cannot always combat illness without medication my doctor is well aware that I do not believe in prescriptions drugs and I try to cure the causes of my illness instead of taking pills. I have been flu free for the last fifteen years and believe in keeping my immune system in the best condition as a way to stay healthy. Yes I also see a massage therapist once every two weeks to help me keep fit and able to work as a therapist myself. I have a male therapist who is sport oriented who works on breaking down my fascia and my treatments are very painful but effective. Along with proper diet and exercise I keep my body balanced and able to do the work massage therapy demands on my physical being.

There are amazing therapists not far from your home. Find out how you can benefit from regular massage treatments when it is coming from the right therapist and environment. The health benefits of massage are wide in rage and if you have coverage then you should be able to benefit from its therapeutic effects. Whether you are trying to relax, or heal an injury or have a more comfortable pregnancy a registered massage therapist can help you with your health needs and give you a proper treatment plan. Maybe you are an athlete who needs to recover from a workout faster or increase your performance either way massage therapy is a great way to achieve different health goals and give you great results with posture and pain or muscle tension.

In The Space Between
Day and Night

The shadows speak
of final hour.
I watch
with weary eyes,
as I gaze
upon the golden sky,
in the space
between day and night.
The wind it cries
of blood and sleep.
I listen
with a bruised soul,
as I strum
my string of dreams
in the space
between day and night.
The sunlight glows
as darkness falls.
I feel, with a faithful heart,
as we dancethe song of hope,
in the space between day and night

CHAPTER NINE

Finding a Top Notch Massage Therapist and Venue

"The greatest wealth is health."

Virgil

Finding a dedicated massage therapist who is dedicated to you and provides great services, is reliable and has some of the following attributes. Here are some of the things to look for in a great massage therapist.

They ask you to fill out a health history form first and make you update it once a year. They give you a proper health assessment and they listen to you and your concerns. If it is your first massage the therapist will make sure you understand procedures and policies before they begin treating you. The massage therapist will ask you the reason for coming in. Is it an injury, or relaxation, where would you like the majority of the treatment to be focused? Is it your legs, back, arms that are giving you problems? Many massage therapists have a massage routine memorized and have not tried to break away doing the same things over and over again not putting the needs of their clients first. A great registered massage therapist keeps educating themselves and taking classes reviewing their anatomy and pathology book to give you a great focused treatment.

You should be able to choose what type of oil or lotion you prefer. Not everyone likes oil on their bodies especially business clients that are heading to the office after their treatment. Oil will stain clothes, and sheets. I prefer using lotion or some gels but will offer all three choices to my clients and allow them to decide for themselves what they want. Some people are allergic to lavender of certain herbs that are used in massage lotions or gels. Tell your massage therapist if you have any allergies to these products.

I do not charge extra for using essential oils but I will always ask my client first if they want a scent being used in their treatment. Some clients do not like scented oils or are very sensitive to any type of smell and for that reason I do not use perfume on myself when I work in my clinic.

Your massage therapist should have a professional attire and demeanor. Their clothes should be proper and not revealing in any way. They wear shoes when they are in a massage room and not bare foot. Many massage therapists will work with no shoes on without realizing that men can get turned on my bare feet. You can tell a lot about your therapist by the effort they make in their grooming. This also means they do not have bad body odor or bad breath when treating you. Their hair is up if it is too long and their hands are washed before your treatment after they massage your feet and when they leave the treatment room.

Music sets the mood in the massage room. I think that the sounds of birds and oceans have been overused the"Oh So Boring New Age CD" that so many people play and annoys for the most part the clients and massage therapist as well. How many clients have asked me if I ever get tired of listening to the same songs over and over again? The truth is I not only get bored with the music that is being played it makes working a torture. A good massage clinic or wellness center can provide you with a choice and selection of massage music. Music can make the massage experience a great one or a bad one. It is not wise to play songs with lyrics as the client will be focusing on the words being played and not relaxing. I had the pleasure of working with massage therapists who thought bringing in their own iPod with heavy rock and folk music was a great idea. Maybe for them but certainly not for the client who later turned around and asked them to "Turn the Shit Off." It never seems to amaze me how many massage therapists and spas really do not understand the value of the aesthetics and music in a room. It is going to affect your return clients, your wages, and your reputation.

A great massage therapist will not indulge in conversation if you do not initiate it first. Some of my clients are nervous and really enjoy talking to me during their treatment but I will always try to encourage them to relax and I respect the needs of my clients by remaining silent and allowing them to fall asleep if they want to. I do check in with them for proper pressure and comfort a few times during the treatment. Do not suffer in silence and not speak your mind if the pressure is too hard or not hard enough and good therapists makes it easy for you to voice your needs.

A great massage therapist is clean and keeps their treatment room safe. This means they wipe down the massage table after every client. It means they take care of their sheets and they make sure that the floors and equipment is clean.

A great massage therapist will make sure you understand their policies and explain them to you over the phone before you have your first appointment. This means cancelation fees, when you need to show up, what to wear if you are getting a Thai massage for example. They will not cut your time by five minutes by giving you a fifty-five minute massage when you booked a one hour appointment. After your massage they will provide you with a treatment plan and proper home care depending on your condition. You should always feel like you can communicate with them and that they are working to make your wellness goal a priority.

A registered massage therapist will provide you with insurance receipts for your treatment so you can claim you massage if you have coverage. The receipts will be under the name of the person who is receiving the massage. They will also not claim to be able to do a treatment or a technique they are not trained or qualified to do. Honesty is the best policy. This also means they do not have gimmicks and charge you extra for a deep tissue or aromatherapy massage.

In general a respectful massage therapist is hard working, looks well dressed and has a professional attitude. Their work space is clean and they take care of themselves and believe in wellness. They also care about your needs and are knowledgeable on the services they provide. They also care about people and are not out to just make a buck at the expense of their client. You feel safe and comfortable with them and you enjoy the benefits of massage. You have found a massage therapist you are happy with in many levels and now you are working on keeping them as your health care professional by forming a long term relationship with them. These registered massage therapist are rewarded by the referrals they received from you to others and have a successful business. Over the years I have herd owners of spas, clinics and wellness centers tell me they have a hard time finding reliable massage therapists and find most of them "Flaky" for lack of better terms. I have worked with irresponsible massage therapists and some of them where flaky, did not dress for success, lacked hygiene, brought their tarot cards into the treatment room and spoke to clients about their horoscope sign. But I also worked with bright professional massage therapists with exceptional hands and skills. Maybe some of these owners should also be looking at what type of pay rate they are offering their massage therapists and maybe that is a good indication why they haven't had any success in keeping and finding the "Sane" ones. You do get what you pay for.

Real success takes team work,dedication, and passion. Without these principals there is no real permanent success and sooner or later what you dish out to the world will come back to haunt you. The cookie cutter spas and resorts will die out eventually because the world will see them for what they really are and the real spiritual institutions will replace them offering better service and real wellness plans making health the priority and not money. The world of aesthetics and massage therapy will no longer collide with each other and massage therapy will be an alternative and healing art being experienced by everyone here in Canada a country who has high standards in massage therapy for the world to follow as well as internationally. We need to look at the definition of the profession to try to make it better and I believe that we will reach these standards in my lifetime. This is how it was meant to be.

ABOUT THE AUTHOR

You can find Irma at www.massageplanetnews.blogspot.com. She is a writer, a journalist and travels extensively to interview people of all walks of life about massage, body work, healing, and artists in general. Irma lives in Toronto and has a new business called *We Got Your Back* and enjoys helping the public gain insight and understanding about massage therapy, what to expect when they go for a treatment for the first time. Her hope is to make massage therapy a profession that is enjoyable and lucrative for the massage therapist and to help people gain understanding into their own healing. Irma is now working on her second book "The Body Panty".

You can also find Irma online on:

http://twitter.com/massageirma

http://facebook.com/massageplanetnews

In A Sacred Place

I hope you hear the sound of waves from different oceans
and find the strength to walk on roads
you have not walked on
Feel a different air on your skin, open
doors you've never seen
I hope you meet new faces and see new sunsets
Walk on foot and travel free
I hope you flow outward like the river meeting the sea
I hope you see the winds of change
blowing fiercely in your land
and let it carry you away from where you stand
away from your fears
and the blinding comfort of your earthly pleasures
I hope you find the heart to seek new treasures
I hope you never give up on life's little surprises,
It is the little surprises that keep
you moving, and evolving,
and becoming....
It is the little surprises that let you
catch a glimpse of my spirit ,
when you realize that wherever your heart goes I am in it
Always... In a sacred place
Where time dissolves, where space dissolves,
What is left is you and me. We are eternity.